Level 1	Part 2

WORKBOOK: HOMEWORK AND CHARACTER BOOK
作业和写字簿

to Accompany

Chinese Link
中文天地
Zhōng Wén Tiān Dì

Elementary Chinese

Simplified Character Version

吴素美 Sue-mei Wu
于月明 Yueming Yu
张燕辉 Yanhui Zhang
田维忠 Weizhong Tian

Carnegie Mellon University

PEARSON Prentice Hall
world Languages
Upper Saddle River, New Jersey 07458

Acquisitions Editor: Rachel McCoy
Publishing Coordinator: Claudia Fernandes
Executive Director of Market Development: Kristine Suárez
Director of Editorial Development: Julia Caballero
Production Supervision: Nancy Stevenson
Project Manager: Margaret Chan, Graphicraft
Assistant Director of Production: Mary Rottino
Supplements Editor: Meriel Martínez Moctezuma
Media Editor: Samantha Alducin
Media Production Manager: Roberto Fernandez
Prepress and Manufacturing Buyer: Christina Helder
Prepress and Manufacturing Assistant Manager: Mary Ann Gloriande
Cover Art Director: Jayne Conte
Marketing Assistant: William J. Bliss
Publisher: Phil Miller
Cover image: Jerry Darvin

This book was set in 12/15 Sabon by Graphicraft Ltd., Hong Kong, and was printed and bound by BRR. The cover was printed by BRR.

PEARSON Prentice Hall

Printed in the United States of America
10 9 8 7 6 5 4

ISBN 0-13-242979-9

Pearson Education Ltd., *London*
Pearson Education Australia Pty, Limited, *Sydney*
Pearson Education Singapore Pte. Ltd.
Pearson Education North Asia Ltd., *Hong Kong*
Pearson Education Canada, Ltd., *Toronto*
Pearson Educación de México, S.A. de C.V.
Pearson Education – Japan, *Tokyo*
Pearson Education Malaysia Pte. Ltd.
Pearson Education, *Upper Saddle River,* New Jersey

目录 CONTENTS

Character Book Indices

Name: ____________________ Date: ______________

拼音作业一 Pinyin Homework I

imple finals: a o e i u ü *Labial initials: b p m f* *Alveolar initials: d t n l*

-1 Listen and circle the right final:

1.	lǖ	lǘ	lǚ	lǜ	5.	dē	dé	dě	dè
2.	fū	fú	fǔ	fù	6.	mō	mó	mǒ	mò
3.	pī	pí	pǐ	pì	7.	tī	tí	tǐ	tì
4.	nā	ná	nǎ	nà	8.	bā	bá	bǎ	bà

-2 Listen and circle the right initial:

1.	mù	nù	4.	lǔ	nǔ	7.	lǚ	nǚ	10.	nǐ	lǐ
2.	pā	tā	5.	pà	bà	8.	bè	tè	11.	tā	lā
3.	mó	fó	6.	tè	lè	9.	dí	tí	12.	pū	mū

-3 Listen and fill in the blanks with the right sound:

1. ______	6. ______	11. ______	16. ______
2. ______	7. ______	12. ______	17. ______
3. ______	8. ______	13. ______	18. ______
4. ______	9. ______	14. ______	19. ______
5. ______	10. ______	15. ______	20. ______

拼音作业二 Pinyin Homework II

Velar initials: g k h *Palatal initials: j q x*
Dental sibilant initials: z c s *Retroflex initials: zh ch sh r*

2-1 Listen and circle the right initial:

1. qì xì	6. zhè zè	11. cǐ sǐ	16. rè chè
2. xī sī	7. jī qī	12. shú chú	17. cā zā
3. shī sī	8. rì shì	13. hù rù	18. gé hé
4. jǐ xǐ	9. zhà chà	14. lè gè	19. cū sū
5. cè chè	10. zǔ sǔ	15. xì shì	20. gē kē

2-2 Listen and fill in the blank with the right initial:

1. ____ē	11. ____à	21. ____é
2. ____ī	12. ____ú	22. ____á
3. ____è	13. ____ǐ	23. ____ě
4. ____ī	14. ____è	24. ____ì
5. ____ā	15. ____ì	25. ____ū
6. ____í	16. ____è	26. ____ǎ
7. ____ù	17. ____ù	27. ____ì
8. ____ì	18. ____è	28. ____ǔ
9. ____ū	19. ____ǐ	29. ____é
10. ____ē	20. ____ì	30. ____ù

Name: ____________________ Date: ______________

拼音作业三 Pinyin Homework III

Compound finals: ai ei ao ou ia iao ie iu ua uo uai ui üe

-1 Listen and mark the right tones:

1. lao	6. hou	11. kuo	16. nuo
2. cui	7. hua	12. pei	17. hui
3. zhua	8. ai	13. shuo	18. biao
4. liu	9. lüe	14. bie	19. tou
5. ren	10. shuai	15. zhou	20. mao

-2 Listen and circle the right sounds:

1.	chóu	zhóu	6.	cáo	cái	11.	jiǎo	xiǎo	16.	bǎo	biǎo
2.	chāo	qiāo	7.	lái	léi	12.	bié	béi	17.	shāo	xiāo
3.	dōu	duō	8.	lín	liú	13.	lüè	nüè	18.	luó	lóu
4.	jué	xué	9.	dāo	dōu	14.	xuē	xiū	19.	guò	gòu
5.	huó	hóu	10.	diū	duī	15.	rào	ròu	20.	jiā	jiē

-3 Listen and fill in the blanks with the right finals:

1. b______	8. l______	15. zh______
2. p______	9. g______	16. ch______
3. m______	10. k______	17. sh______
4. f ______	11. h______	18. r______
5. d______	12. j______	19. z______
6. t______	13. q______	20. c______
7. n______	14. x______	21. s______

拼音作业四 Pinyin Homework IV

Nasal finals: *an en* *ian in* *uan un*
ang eng ong *iang ing iong* *uang*

4-1 Listen and mark the right tones:

1. jiong	6. lun	11. hen	16. nuan
2. xian	7. rong	12. qiang	17. zhuang
3. hun	8. fen	13. heng	18. zhun
4. an	9. cang	14. liang	19. sun
5. qin	10. mian	15. ling	20. ding

4-2 Listen and circle the right sounds:

1. juān	jūn	6. lín	líng	11. xióng	qióng	16. cóng	chóng
2. zhèn	shèn	7. tūn	tuān	12. zhàn	zhèn	17. zhāng	jiāng
3. qiáng	qióng	8. rēng	zhēng	13. háng	huáng	18. xūn	sūn
4. xiàng	xuàn	9. kàn	kèn	14. huán	huáng	19. gèn	gèng
5. rǎn	zhǎn	10. qǐng	xǐng	15. jūn	qūn	20. nián	lián

4-3 Listen and fill in the blanks with the right finals:

1. b______	8. l______	15. zh______
2. p______	9. g______	16. ch______
3. m______	10. k______	17. sh______
4. f______	11. h______	18. r______
5. d______	12. j______	19. z______
6. t______	13. q______	20. c______
7. n______	14. x______	21. s______

Name: ________________ Date: ____________

拼音作业五 Pinyin Homework V

Special Pinyin and tonal rules

5-1 Listen and fill in the blanks with the right Pinyin:

1. ______ 6. ______ 11. ______ 16. ______

2. ______ 7. ______ 12. ______ 17. ______

3. ______ 8. ______ 13. ______ 18. ______

4. ______ 9. ______ 14. ______ 19. ______

5. ______ 10. ______ 15. ______ 20. ______

5-2 Mark the tones of "yi" (一) and "bu" (不) in accordance with the "yi-bu" tonal rules:

1. ____wǔ____shí
   一五一十

2. ____xīn____yì
   一心一意

3. ____zhāo____xī
   一朝一夕

4. ____chàng____hè
   一唱一和

5. ____mó____yàng
   一模一样

6. ____wén____wèn
   不闻不问

7. ____míng____bái
   不明不白

8. ____zhé____kòu
   不折不扣

9. ____sān____sì
   不三不四

10. ____bēi____kàng
    不卑不亢

11. ____ sī____gǒu
    一丝不苟

12. ____ chéng____biàn
    一成不变

13. ____wén____zhí
    一文不值

14. ____qiào____tōng
    一窍不通

15. ____chén____rǎn
    一尘不染

拼音作业六 Pinyin Homework VI

Comprehensive Pinyin Review

6-1 Listen and circle the right sounds:

1.	dàng	dèng	6.	lǚ	liǔ	11.	yǔ	yǒu	16.	zhàn	jiàn
2.	lǚ	nǚ	7.	bīn	bīng	12.	lián	liáng	17.	yuǎn	yǎn
3.	wō	ōu	8.	niè	lèi	13.	xiōng	jiōng	18.	jiǎo	xiǎo
4.	jié	zéi	9.	dōu	tōu	14.	kǒu	gǒu	19.	xiù	shòu
5.	jūn	zhēn	10.	zuō	cuō	15.	xià	xiào	20.	cāi	sāi

6-2 Listen to the following classroom expressions. Then write them in Pinyin:

1. ______________________________

2. ______________________________

3. ______________________________

4. ______________________________

5. ______________________________

6. ______________________________

7. ______________________________

8. ______________________________

9. ______________________________

10. ______________________________

Name: ____________________ Date: ______________

Lesson 11 Do You Want Black Tea or Green Tea?

. Listening Exercises

. Listen to the dialogue and mark the correct statements with "✓" and the incorrect ones with "✗":

☐ 1. 小美和于英正在法国饭馆吃饭。

☐ 2. 小美正在喝汤。

☐ 3. 饭馆的牛肉很好吃。

☐ 4. 于英不喜欢喝可乐。

. Listen to the telephone conversation between 方小文 and a waitress in a Chinese restaurant. Check the items and circle the numbers 方小文 has ordered for pick-up.

Note: 拿 [ná]: pick up

方小文点的菜：

☐ 啤酒 1 2 3 4 5

☐ 可乐 1 2 3 4 5

☐ 冰红茶 1 2 3 4 5

☐ 汤 1 2 3 4 5

☐ 炒饭 1 2 3 4 5
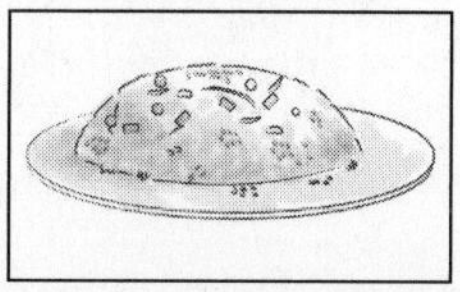

☐ 炒面 1 2 3 4 5

☐ 饺子 10 20 30 40 50

II. Character Exercises

A. Write the characters for the following words:

1. xǐhuān

2. háishì

3. píjiǔ

4. lǜchá

5. chǎomiàn

6. kělè

7. chǎofàn

8. xiǎng

9. fànguǎn

10. bīnghóngchá

11. xiānsheng

12. xiǎojiě

13. fúwùyuán

14. jiǎozi

15. shuāng

16. pán

Name: __________________ Date: ______________

3. Write out the radicals for the following characters, count their stroke numbers, and look up their meanings in the dictionary and enter on chart:

Characters	Radical	No. of strokes	Definition
馆	饣	11	house
务			
坐			
员			
喝			
茶			
杯			
红			
冰			
乐			
瓶			
酒			
盘			
面			
筷			

III. Grammar Exercises

A. Ask an alternative question based on the choices given and then answer it:

1. 吃中国菜，吃法国菜

____?

____

2. 去打球，去图书馆

____?

____

3. 两点下课，三点下课

____?

____

4. 是工程师，是老师

____?

____

5. 有四门课，有五门课

____?

____

Name: ________________ Date: ____________

B. Fill in the blanks with the proper measure words (some of them may be used more than once):

位　只　个　杯　瓶　辆　盘　碗　双　本

1. 常先生是一 ___ 很好的老师。
2. 我点两 ___ 炒饭和两 ___ 可乐。
3. 爸爸有一 ___ 狗。
4. 我们家有四 ___ 人。
5. 她想喝一 ___ 茶。
6. 我的朋友要一 ___ 啤酒。
7. 那个美国人有一 ___ 车。
8. 那三 ___ 法国人想喝一 ___ 冰红茶和两 ___ 咖啡。
9. 这五 ___ 学生有三 ___ 工程书。
10. 给我们三 ___ 汤和一 ___ 筷子。

C. Translate the following sentences into Chinese:

1. Do you like drinking tea or coffee?

____

2. Which subject do you like to study, literature or engineering?

____

3. After eating the fried rice, I want to drink a cup of tea.

____

4. I often go to Chinese restaurants.

____

IV. Comprehensive Exercises

Three old friends of yours are coming to your apartment for a visit in the evening. But you are unfortunately unable to prepare food for them. You leave a note to your roommate and ask him/her to do you a favor by ordering food from the Chinese restaurant (at least 70 characters). Please include the following words and phrases in the note:

点 要 想 喜欢 杯 瓶 盘 碗 双 谢谢

Name: ____________________ Date: ______________

Lesson 12 May I Borrow Your Car?

. Listening Exercises

A. Listen to the following sentences, fill in the blanks, and then translate the sentences into English:

1. 他 ___ 知道我 ___ 不 ___ 在他的家吃晚饭。

____

2. 你 ___ ___ 少喝一点儿咖啡。

____

3. 小李 ___ 开车去学校的图书馆 ___ 两本 ___ ___ ___ ___ 书。

____

4. ___ 纽约开车 ___ 洛杉矶 ___ ___ 五天。

____

5. 今年五月我 ___ 回家看妈妈。

____

6. 我明天 ___ ___ 用我朋友 ___ ___ 我的电脑 ___ 小王写电子邮件。

____

Notes: 纽约 [Niǔyuē]: New York
洛杉矶 [Luòshānjī]: Los Angeles
电脑 [diànnǎo]: computer

B. Listen to the dialogue between 方明英 and 丁文, and then mark the correct statements with "✓" and the incorrect ones with "✗":

☐ 1. 丁明很想看这个中国电影。

☐ 2. 丁文明天下午没有课。

☐ 3. 每天下午有车从宿舍到中美图书馆。

☐ 4. 丁文要跟方明英一起看电影。

Note: 电影 [diànyǐng]: movie

II. Character Exercises

A. Comprehensive character exercises:

Process 1: Write down the radical.

Process 2: Count strokes of the character.

Process 3: Write down the correct Pinyin for the character.

Process 4: Make as many words or phrases with the character as you can.

Example: 机 → 木 → 6 → jī → 计算机、手机、飞机、机场

	Radical	No. of strokes	Pinyin	Word
1. 场				
2. 习				
3. 进				
4. 样				

B. Circle all the simplified characters in the following dialogue and then provide their traditional forms:

王家欢：于飞，你的电脑可以看中文，是吗？

于　飞：对，有什么事儿吗？

王家欢：我要上网找中文资料，可以借你的电脑用一下儿吗？

于　飞：没问题。现在我不用电脑，可是吃饭以后我要用电脑做作业。

王家欢：知道了，谢谢！

于　飞：不客气。

Notes: 找 [zhǎo]: look for
资料 [zīliào]: material

1. ______ 2. ______ 3. ______ 4. ______ 5. ______

6. ______ 7. ______ 8. ______ 9. ______ 10. ______

11. ______ 12. ______ 13. ______ 14. ______ 15. ______

Name: ________________ Date: ____________

III. Grammar Exercises

A. Fill in the blanks with the following optative words:

要，想，应该，得，能，可以，会

1. 他们 _____ 坐飞机从纽约来这儿玩儿。
2. 我的爸爸妈妈都 _____ 说中文，你 _____ _____ 跟他们说中文。
3. 她 _____ _____ 会开手排挡的车。
4. 我今天晚上 _____ 借你的车吗?

B. Write the negations of the following sentences:

1. 我要在早上六点起床。

____

2. 我们想多喝点茶。

____

3. 小美应该多练习开车。

____

4. 我能借老师的书。

____

5. 在宿舍可以看电视。

____

6. 老师今天会晚点儿下课。

____

7. 你得开车去机场。

____

C. Translate the following sentences into Chinese:

1. I want to borrow a Chinese novel from the library, but I don't know which one is good.

    ____

2. Can you give a brief introduction about Shanghai?

    ____

3. I can speak Chinese, know a lot of characters, and can write a little Chinese.

    ____

4. What will you do after you are back in your dormitory?

    ____

IV. Comprehensive Exercises

Read the following passage and answer the questions which follow:

我叫李红英，我在华中大学学工程。我的爸爸妈妈都是中国人，可是我在美国出生，也在美国长大 [zhǎngdà] (grow up)。我小的时候，爸爸妈妈说我应该学中文。可是我不喜欢学中文。爸爸妈妈跟我说中文的时候，我总是 [zǒngshì] (always) 跟他们说英文。

上大学以后我认识到 [rènshidào] (realize) 学中文很重要，于是 [yúshì] (therefore) 我非常想学中文了。去年八月的时候，我去问 [wèn] (ask) 华中大学中文系的王老师我应该上哪个中文班。王老师问我的中文怎么样。我说我能说一点儿中文，可是我一个中文字也不会写。王老师说我应该在一年级 [yī niánjí] (Grade One) 学中文。

我从去年九月到十二月在华中大学学中文。现在我已经 [yǐjīng] (already) 能说很多句子，还能读，也能写二百五十个中文字了。

这个学期我要继续学中文。今年夏天 [xiàtiān] (summer) 我想去中国学习，这样就能多跟中国人说中文，我的中文也一定 [yídìng] (must) 能进步。

1. 李红英在哪个大学学习？她的专业 [zhuānyè] (major) 是什么？

____

2. 李红英小的时候跟爸爸妈妈说中文吗？

____

3. 上中文课以前，李红英会说中文、写中文吗？

____

4. 王老师说李红英应该上哪个中文班？

____

5. 李红英是从去年几月到几月在大学学习中文的？

____

6. 今年夏天李红英要做什么？

____

Name: ________________ Date: ____________

Lesson 13 I Want to Buy a Shirt

I. Listening Exercises

A. Listen to the dialogue and read the following statements. Mark the correct statements with "✓" and the incorrect ones with "✗".

☐ 1. 方明飞想买一件衬衫。

☐ 2. 店员要他试试蓝色的牛仔裤。

☐ 3. 方明飞喜欢黑色的牛仔裤。

☐ 4. 店员说黄衬衫很好看。

☐ 5. 方明飞说黑色的衬衫很不错。

B. Listen to the statements and fill in the blanks with appropriate words:

1. 我想买一____衬衫________一条裤子。

2. 你________看看。我______这件好吗?

3. 这条裙子__________?

4. 请__________。

5. 我________喜欢黑色的。

II. Character Exercises

A. Circle all the simplified characters in the following dialogue and then provide their traditional forms:

钱　飞：小天，你帮我看看，我穿这件衬衫怎么样？

张小天：我觉得那件黄的好看。这件黑的不太好看。

钱　飞：好，我试试那件黄的。不错，我很喜欢。你呢？你想买什么？

张小天：我想买一条裙子或者一条裤子。

钱　飞：裙子和裤子都买吧。

张小天：好，我都买。

1. ______ 2. ______ 3. ______ 4. ______ 5. ______

6. ______ 7. ______ 8. ______ 9. ______ 10. ______

11. ______ 12. ______ 13. ______ 14. ______ 15. ______

B. Write the characters for the following Pinyin words and group them according to their radicals in the chart provided:

1. wèi ______ 2. chuān ______ 3. tiáo ______ 4. mǎi ______

5. qún ______ 6. ràng ______ 7. shì ______ 8. shān ______

9. chèn ______ 10. jiā ______ 11. jiàn ______ 12. yuán ______

Group no.	Radical	Characters with the radical
1		
2		
3		
4		
5		
6		
7		
8		

Name: ____________ Date: ____________

III. Grammar Exercises

A. Fill in each blank with an appropriate measure word:

1. 一 ________ 裤子	2. 两 ________ 衬衫
3. 三 ________ 鞋	4. 四 ________ 裙子
5. 五 ________ 牛仔裤	6. 六 ________ 运动衫
7. 七 ________ 小狗	8. 八 ________ 电影票

B. Complete the following dialogues based on the clues given:

1. 你说那件衬衫怎么样?

   ______________________________ 。
   (Let me have a look.)

2. 我应该穿几号的?

   ______________________________ 。
   (Try size 6 or size 7.)

3. 我不知道这个电影是说什么的。

   ______________________________ 。
   (I'll give you a little introduction.)

4. 上海春卷真好吃。

   真的吗? ______________________________ 。
   (I'll taste it as well.)

5. 手排挡的车我还不会开。

   ______________________________ 。
   (You should learn it.)

C. Answer the following questions using the expression "或者":

1. 你想买什么?

____

2. 这张电影票是谁的?

____

3. 我们去哪个餐馆吃饭?

____

4. 你喜欢黄衬衫吗?

____

IV. Comprehensive Exercises

Describe a recent shopping trip (about 80–100 characters).

____

____

____

____

____

____

____

____

Name: ________________ Date: ____________

Lesson 14 I Am 20 This Year

I. Listening Exercises

A. Listen to the sentences and fill in the blanks with the missing characters:

1. 三月十八日是我的 __________ 。

2. 我今年 __________，__________ 二十岁。

3. __________ 是我的生日 __________。请你 __________。

B. Listen to the dialogue, then mark the correct statements with "✓" and the incorrect ones with "✗":

☐ 1. 星星今年二十岁。

☐ 2. 明明下个星期五要过生日。

☐ 3. 星星下个星期五晚上没有空。

☐ 4. 方明明的妈妈要做一个蛋糕。

☐ 5. 方明明要吃两块蛋糕。

II. Character Exercises

A. Following are the characters from the lesson. For each one:

1. Identify the radical.
2. Count the number of strokes.
3. Give the English definition.
4. Provide more characters with the same radical.

Character	Radical	No. of strokes	English	More examples
家				
送				
地				
星				
棒				

B. Write the following Pinyin sentences in Chinese characters:

1. Wǒde shēngrì shì yīyuè sān shí hào, xīngqīsì.

____

2. Zhè shì nǐde péngyou sòng nǐde dà dàngāo ma?

____

3. Nǐ jīnnián duō dà? Wǒ jīnnián shíjiǔ suì.

____

III. Grammar Exercises

A. Find the following dates from this year's calendar and fill in the blanks:

1. 今年春节 [Chūnjié] (Spring Festival / Chinese New Year) 是 __________ (date), __________ (weekday) 。

2. 今天是 __________ (date), __________ (weekday) 。

3. 下个星期日是 __________ (date) 。

4. 今年的感恩节 [Gǎn'ēnjié] (Thanksgiving) 是 ________ (date) __________(weekday) 。

5. 圣诞节 [Shèngdànjié] (Christmas) 是 __________ (date) __________ (weekday) 。

6. 我的生日是 __________ (date), 今年在 __________ (weekday) 。

Name: ________________ Date: ____________

B. Complete the following sentences with the help of the clues:

1. 下个星期日我要 ____ 。
   (to hold a birthday party for my boyfriend)

2. 你可以 ____ ?
   (to make an order of Chinese dumplings for me)

3. 后天是妈妈的生日，我要 ________________________________ 。
   (to buy a very pretty shirt for her)

IV. Comprehensive Exercises

Make a telephone call to your friend inviting him/her to attend your boyfriend's birthday party next Saturday. You will need to include (but are not limited to) the following words and expressions:

生日　空　晚会　月　号　还是　为　参加　知道　地址

Name: ____________________ Date: ______________

Lesson 15 The Library Is in Front of the Dorm

I. Listening Exercises

A. Liang Zhi is giving you a brief introduction of his dorm. Listen carefully and then draw a floor plan based on what you hear:

B. Answer the following questions based on this floor plan:

1. 梁志的宿舍在哪儿?

2. 他的宿舍里边有什么?

3. 客厅的右边是什么?

4. 餐厅在厨房的哪边?

5. 宿舍的对面是什么?

II. Character Exercises

A. Circle characters that have both traditional and simplified forms. Write the traditional/simplified character pairs in the numbered spaces below the dialogue:

常飞：方园，你的宿舍在哪儿？

方园：我的宿舍在学校旁边。

常飞：你的宿舍有几个卧室？你有室友吗？

方园：有两个卧室。田真是我的室友。他的房间在右边，我的在左边。

常飞：你们宿舍有客厅吗？

方园：有一个客厅，还有一个餐厅。

常飞：有没有厨房？

方园：我们有厨房，是公用的。我们的宿舍很不错，你来看看吧。

1. ______ 2. ______ 3. ______ 4. ______ 5. ______ 6. ______

7. ______ 8. ______ 9. ______ 10. ______ 11. ______ 12. ______

13. ______ 14. ______ 15. ______ 16. ______ 17. ______

Name: ____________________ Date: ______________

II. Grammar Exercises

A. Here is a floor plan of an apartment in the new dorm. Look at it and answer the following questions:

Note: 走廊 [zǒuláng]: hallway

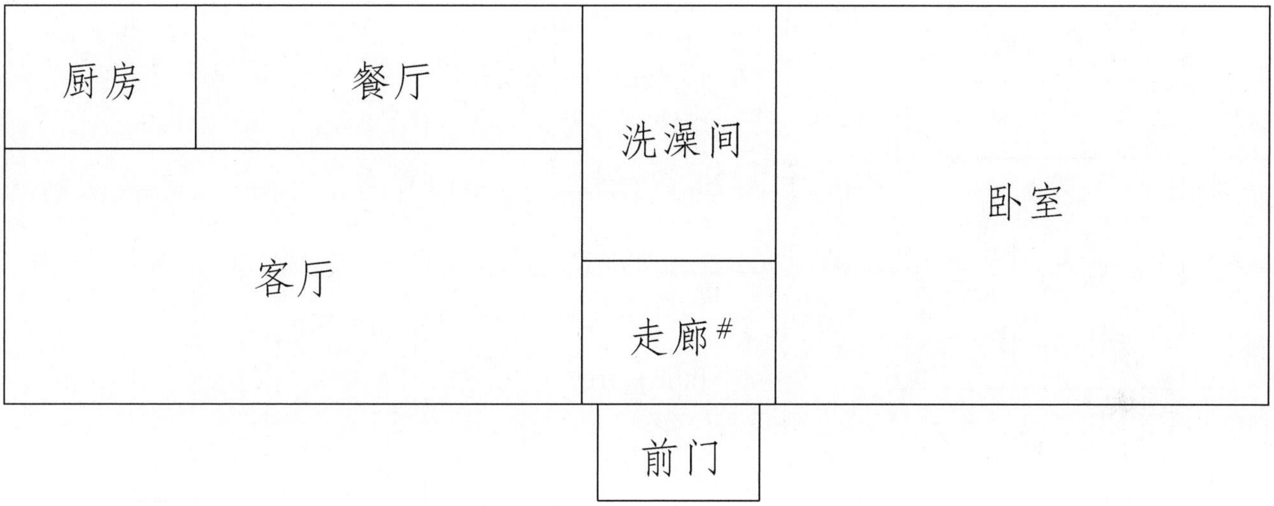

1. 卧室在哪儿？

____

2. 卧室的对面是什么？

____

3. 厨房和洗澡间的中间是什么？

____

4. 客厅和卧室的中间有什么？

____

5. 餐厅在客厅的哪边？

____

B. Fill in the blanks with 有，在，是 with the help of the pictures:

1. 

裙子 ______ 鞋的右边。

裙子的左边 ______ 鞋。

Notes: 右边 [yòubiān]: right

左边 [zuǒbiān]: left

2. 

房子的后边 ______ 一棵树。

房子 ______ 树的前边。

Notes: 棵 [kē]: measure word for plants

树 [shù]: tree

3. 

球的左边 ______ 一件衬衫，鞋 ______ 球的下边。

衬衫 ______ 球的左边，球的下边 ______ 鞋。

IV. Comprehensive Exercises

You are learning about housing in the U.S. Each of you is required to give a short talk to your class about your house. You are now preparing for the talk. Write out what you want to say in your introduction. Use as many words and expressions as possible from the text. The following expressions can be used as well:

大门	[dàmén]	main gate	楼梯	[lóutī]	stairs
车库	[chēkù]	garage	院子	[yuànzi]	(court)yard
地下室	[dìxiàshì]	basement			

___

___

___

___

Name: ____________ Date: ____________

Lesson 16 She Plays Basketball Very Well

I. Listening Exercises

A. Listen to the dialogue and fill in the blanks based on what you hear:

爱文：信美，你喜欢什么 ________?

信美：我喜欢打球。我 ____________________。

爱文：是吗？我也喜欢打球，可是我喜欢打排球。我排球

____________。

信美：你 ____________ 怎么样? 我 ________ 不太好。我得多练习练习。

爱文：我 ____________ 马马虎虎 [mǎmǎhūhū]。我也得多练习。

Notes: 运动 [yùndòng]: sports, exercises

马马虎虎 [mǎmǎhūhū]: just so-so

B. Listen to the sentences and choose the correct answer:

1. a. 小美做饭做得很慢。
   b. 小美吃饭吃得很慢。
2. a. 欢欢篮球打得不太好。
   b. 欢欢篮球打得太好了。
3. a. 正然作业做得很快、很好。
   b. 正然写字写得很好。

II. Character Exercises

A. Match the traditional form of the characters with their simplified forms:

鍛 籃 體 圖 邊 業 廳

篮 体 边 厅 图 锻 业

B. Find from the lesson the characters with the following radicals:

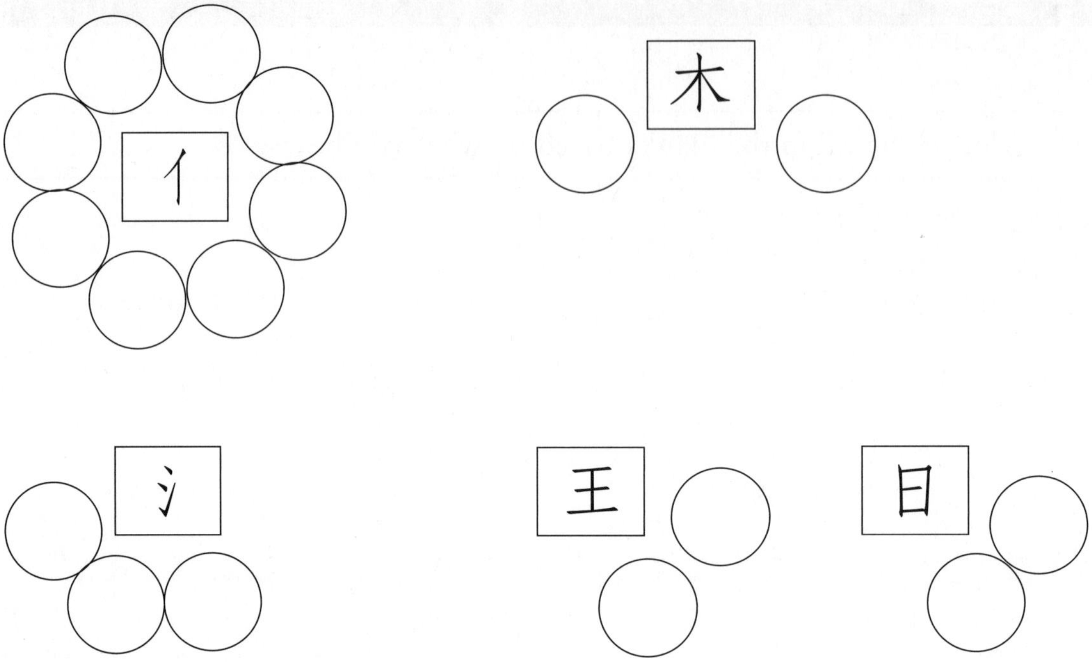

III. Grammar Exercises

A. Translate the following into Chinese:

1. He came very early.

    ____

2. I often eat very slowly.

    ____

3. You walk too fast.

    ____

4. He plays basketball very well.

    ____

5. My roommate goes to bed very late.

    ____

6. My mom makes dumplings very fast.

    ____

Name: ____________________ Date: ______________

B. Rewrite the following sentences with emphasis on the object of each sentence:

1. 她打篮球打得不错。

____

2. 妈妈包饺子包得非常快。

____

3. 谁做饭做得很好?

____

4. 我睡觉睡得太少。

____

IV. Comprehensive Exercises

A. Read the following paragraph and then answer the questions. Look up the new words in a dictionary when needed:

包健和杨中是室友。他们俩都非常喜欢运动,常常一起去健身房锻炼。包健游泳游得特别好,他是学校游泳队的队长,他也是杨中的游泳教练。杨中游得也不错,可是他不常常游泳。

他喜欢打球,特别是篮球,他打得非常好,投球投得特别准。他也喜欢打排球、乒乓球。排球、乒乓球他都打得不错。他是学校篮球队的中锋,每次比赛他都要参加。

他们俩不但喜欢运动,而且还喜欢做饭。包健包饺子包得很快,也很好看。杨中做中国菜做得特别好吃。他们也常常请同学们去他们的宿舍吃饭。同学们常常吃得很多,吃得太饱了。

Notes: 队 [duì]: team
队长 [duìzhǎng]: team leader
特别 [tèbié]: especially
投 [tóu]: throw
准 [zhǔn]: accurate
乒乓球 [pīngpāngqiú]: table tennis
中锋 [zhōngfēng]: center (in basketball game)
不但……而且……[búdàn …… érqiě ……]: not only . . . but also . . .
饱 [bǎo]: full

Questions:

1. 包健和杨中常常去哪儿?

____

2. 包健什么特别好? 杨中呢?

____

3. 杨中喜欢什么运动?

____

4. 他们俩做饭做得怎么样?

____

5. 同学们常常去他们宿舍做什么?

____

B. Change the above paragraph into a dialogue between 包健 and 杨中:

____

____

____

____

____

Name: ______________ Date: ____________

Lesson 17 Spring Is Coming Soon

. Listening Exercises

. Listen and fill in the blanks, then translate them into English:

1. ______ 就要来了，天气很快就要 ___ 了。

   ____

2. 有 ______ 我会去 ______ 玩玩。

   ____

3. 我很喜欢吃中国菜，______ 我最喜欢吃牛肉面。

   ____

4. 这两天 ____________，我想去游泳池游泳。你也去吗？

   ____

5. 我学习不太忙 ____________，就跟你一起去看电影。

   ____

6. 这个学期就要 ___ 了，我们很快就要 ___ 春假了。

   ____

. Listen to the dialogue between 夏华 and 春红, then mark the correct statements with "✓" and the incorrect ones with "✗":

- [ ] 1. 春红这个学期不忙。
- [ ] 2. 春红就要参加学校的篮球赛了。
- [ ] 3. 夏华在春假的时候要回家。
- [ ] 4. 夏华就要和她的好朋友见面了。

II. Character Exercises

A. Write out the characters for the following Pinyin:

1. chūntiān		2. qìhòu		3. dōngtiān	
4. rèjíle		5. dù		6. fàngjià	
7. nuǎnhuo		8. xiàyǔ		9. zuì	
10. shíjiān		11. huáshì		12. xiàxuě	
13. qízhōng		14. guāfēng		15. hǎojiǔbújiàn	
16. jiànmiàn					

B. Find the radicals in the following characters, indicate their numbers of strokes, and then write their definitions from an English dictionary:

Characters	Radical	No. of strokes	Definition
春	日	9	spring
夏			
秋			
冬			
气			
最			
暖			
热			
短			
度			
极			
风			
雪			

Name: ________________ Date: ____________

III. Grammar Exercises

A. Select an appropriate pattern from the list and place it correctly in the sentence:

……的时候，就要/快要……了，其中

1. 我有一辆白色的车。

____

2. 她的弟弟今年十八岁。

____

3. 这个学期我有五门课。我最喜欢中文课。

____

4. 开车不应该打手机。

____

B. Read the following passage and fill in the blanks with appropriate words or phrases:

下个月是三月，我们很快_____要_____春假了。春假的_____ _____，我和我的室友小玲要去加拿大的多伦多 [Duōlúnduō] (Toronto) 玩。明天下午我和小玲_____没有课，我们想一起去商店 [shāngdiàn] (store) 买要去加拿大穿的衣服。小玲说她想买一条裙子，我说不好。多伦多的三月_____ _____ _____会非常冷，最冷的_____ _____才华氏三十度，冷_____了。我说买一条牛仔裤怎么样，她说很好。我想买一_____鞋。商店里皮鞋、球鞋和靴子_____在减价 [jiǎnjià] (on sale)，_____ _____我最想买一双球鞋。我们很快就_____去旅行 [lǚxíng] (travel) 了，我高兴_____了！

C. Translate the following sentences into Chinese:

1. I will eat the Chinese food cooked by my mother soon.

   ____

2. They will attend the soccer game soon.

   ____

3. I like sports. Among the sports I like, I enjoy playing basketball the most.

   ____

4. Sometimes she uses chopsticks to eat.

   ____

5. This birthday cake is extremely delicious.

   ____

IV. Comprehensive Exercises

Write an essay describing the climate of the place where you come from (at least 100 characters).

Please include the following words and phrases:

……的时候，就要/快要……了，其中，最，极了，华氏/摄氏

____

____

____

____

____

____

Name: ____________ Date: ____________

Lesson 18 We Are Going to Take a Train Trip

I. Listening Exercises

A. Listen to the dialogue and read the statements below. Mark a "✓" for a correct statement and a "✗" for an incorrect one. Write out the correct answer for the wrong statement:

☐ 1. 文健春假要去看他的爷爷奶奶。 ____________

☐ 2. 小华春假要去佛罗里达。 ____________

☐ 3. 文健的爸爸妈妈住在洛杉矶。 ____________

☐ 4. 小华要和朋友一起开车去玩儿。 ____________

☐ 5. 文健和妹妹都喜欢去海边游泳。 ____________

Notes: 爷爷 [yéye]: grandpa

奶奶 [nǎinai]: grandma

佛罗里达 [Fóluólǐdá]: Florida

B. Listen to the questions and then give answers based on your actual situation:

1. ____________

2. ____________

3. ____________

4. ____________

5. ____________

II. Character Exercises

A. Listen to the above dialogue again and write it down in characters:

____

____

____

____

____

____

____

____

B. Read the dialogue you have written, circle all the characters that have a simplified/traditional form, and provide them below:

Example: 车 (車)

______ ______ ______ ______ ______ ______

______ ______ ______ ______ ______ ______

______ ______ ______ ______ ______

Name: ________________ Date: ____________

I. Grammar Exercises

. Ask a question on each pair of words given below and then answer it according to the requirements for each sentence:

1. Use "离" *Requirement*

   Hint: 教室 [jiàoshì] classroom (健身房) (教室)

   ____

   ____

2. Talk about means of transportation *Requirement*

   Hint: 华盛顿 [Huáshèngdùn]: Washington (纽约) (华盛顿)

   ____

   ____

3. Indicating sequence *Requirement*

   Hint: 商店 [shāngdiàn]: retail store (商店) (公园)

   ____

   ____

4. Use "近" or "远" *Requirement*

   (图书馆) (停车场)

   ____

   ____

The following are the things 文健 is going to do tomorrow. Divide these things into three groups: things to be done in the morning, afternoon, and evening. Arrange them properly, put them into sentences, and then use 先, 再, and 然后 to connect them:

看朋友 游泳 做功课 去买东西 吃早饭

上课 上网 去图书馆 打电话

Note: 东西 [dōngxi]: things

C. Complete the following sentences with a verb phrase based on the artwork clues:

1. 从美国去中国，你得 ________________。

2. 春假她要 ___________ 回家看爸爸妈妈。

3. *A*: 我们怎么去这个饭馆?

   B: 我们坐 _________________ 去。

4. *A*: 你会 _________________ 吗?

   B: 不会。我会 _____________。

IV. Comprehensive Exercises

You are in the dorm chatting with your roommate about your plan for the coming summer. Write a paragraph about your plan beginning with the following sentence. You need to include where you are going, what you are going to do, and what transportation you will use.

我们就要放暑假了……

Name: ______________ Date: ____________

Lesson 19 I Caught a Cold

Listening Exercises

. Listen to the dialogue between 黄飞 and 白雪, and mark the correct statements with "✓" and the incorrect ones with "✗":

☐ 1. 白雪来美国三个月了。

☐ 2. 白雪刚刚 [gāng gāng] (just; a short while ago) 来美国的时候喜欢吃美国菜。

☐ 3. 白雪生病以后去看医生了。

☐ 4. 白雪现在没有生病了。

☐ 5. 白雪现在不喜欢吃美国菜了。

☐ 6. 白雪现在还不会做美国菜。

. Listen to the dialogue between 田小西 and 程小东, and mark the correct statements with "✓" and the incorrect ones with "✗":

☐ 1. 小东上个月买了一辆车。

☐ 2. 小西会开车。

☐ 3. 坐公共汽车要一个半小时才能到学校。

☐ 4. 小东说有时候开车只要五分钟就能到学校了。

II. Character Exercises

A. Write the characters for the following Pinyin:

1. hǎoxiàng
2. gǎnmào
3. bǐjì
4. fùxí
5. shūfu
6. zhǔnbèi
7. gǎnxiè
8. kǎoshì
9. suǒyǐ
10. yīshēng
11. chīyào
12. fāshāo
13. késòu
14. shēngbìng
15. xiūxi
16. tóuténg

B. Write the components of the following characters and circle the radical:

Example: 饿 ㇀ ⓣ + 我

1. 感 ______
2. 像 ______
3. 医 ______
4. 药 ______
5. 准 ______
6. 笔 ______
7. 复 ______
8. 发 ______

Name: ____________ Date: ____________

II. Grammar Exercises

A. Change the following sentences to questions, then give a negative answer to each question:

1. 这个夏天我就要去北京学中文了。

Question: ____________

Negative answer: ____________

2. 她做了两个蛋糕。

Question: ____________

Negative answer: ____________

3. 我下了课以后，就去图书馆看书。

Question: ____________

Negative answer: ____________

4. 昨天我在我朋友家喝了很多酒。

Question: ____________

Negative answer: ____________

B. Translate the following sentences into Chinese:

1. I bought that red skirt tonight.

____

2. Let's go swimming together after you recover from your illness.

____

3. I haven't eaten for the whole day today. Therefore, I feel very hungry now.

____

4. He has read three Chinese novels.

____

5. I traveled to the West during the spring break.

____

IV. Comprehensive Exercises

Guided composition:

You have been staying up very late for several days and have caught a cold. You felt too sick to attend Chinese class today. Please write an excuse note to the teacher. Your classmate will bring the note to your Chinese teacher.

Write the note according to the following format. (Write at least 80 characters)

______老师：

____

____

____

____

____

____

____

____

学生：(你的名字

(　　年　　月　　日

Name: ________________ Date: ____________

Lesson 20 I've Brought Xiao Xie Over . . .

Listening Exercises

. Listen and write the Pinyin for the following expressions:

1. 我想搬出去住。 ________________
2. 我把我女朋友带来了。 ________________
3. 每个月的第一天必须付房租。 ________________
4. 请你马上下来。 ________________

. Listen to the dialogue and mark the correct statements with "✓" and the incorrect ones with "✗":

☐ 1. 那是小明的公寓，他们先在外面，然后进去。

☐ 2. 那是小明的电视，他从家里搬过来的。

☐ 3. 小谢把房租带来了。

☐ 4. 房东太太住在楼上。

☐ 5. 小明跑上楼去把中文书给房东太太。

Note: 房东太太 [fáng dōng tàitai]: landlady

. Character Exercises

. For each character, make two phrases, write down the Pinyin, and make a few sentences:

搬	搬下去 搬下来	bānshàngqù bānxiàlái	你想把桌子搬下去吗? 是的，我想把桌子搬下来。
带			
楼			
烟			

B. Write down the radical of each of the following characters and provide the meaning of th radical. List at least five characters that have the same radical:

Example: 吗 口 mouth 呢 喝 吃 和 啊

1. 回 ______________________________

2. 搬 ______________________________

3. 饭 ______________________________

4. 但 ______________________________

5. 楼 ______________________________

III. Grammar Exercises

A. __Situation:__ 明学's Mom is coming to visit him the day after tomorrow. This is their phone conversation.

1. Fill in the blanks with 把 and a directional complement:

明学：喂，是妈妈吗？我是明学。你后天 _____ 我的车 _____ _____ _____ 的时候 (drive my car over)，也 _____ 我的电脑 _____ _____ _____ (move my computer over)，好吗？

妈妈：可以，要不要也 _____ 你的夏天衣服 _____ _____ _____ (bring your summer clothes over) 呢？

明学：也好，一定要 _____ 那件黄衬衫 _____ _____ _____ (bring it over)，我很喜欢那件。

妈妈：没问题。噢！对了，爸爸给你买了一个新手机。

明学：太好了！请 _____ 那个新手机也 _____ _____ _____ (bring it over) 给我吧！

妈 妈：我今天做了饺子，要不要也 _____ 一些 _____ _____ (bring some over) 呢？

明 学：太好了，我的室友要 _____ _____ _____ 了 (move out)，他很喜欢吃饺子，你多拿一些 _____ _____ (take some over)，可以请他也尝尝 [chángchang] (have a taste of)。

妈 妈：那我就多 _____ 一 些 _____ _____ (take some over)。

明 学：妈，我好困 [kùn] (sleepy) 哦！(I am very sleepy!) 我想再回 _____ (go back) 睡觉。

妈 妈：你昨天晚上是什么时候从学校回 _____ (go back) 的？

明 学：我没有车，我是 _____ _____ _____ 的 (walk back)，十一点半才 _____ _____ (come back)。再见！

. Answer the following questions in Chinese (use 把 and/or directional complements):

1. 明学的妈妈什么时候过去看他？

____

2. 妈妈要带什么过去？

____

3. 明学要妈妈把黄衬衫怎么样？

____

4. 新手机是谁买的？要怎么处理 [chǔlǐ] (deal with) 呢？

____

5. 明学昨天晚上是什么时候回去的？

____

IV. Comprehensive Exercises

Translate the following passage into English (paying attention to the usage of 把 and directional complements).

刻舟求剑 [kè zhōu qiú jiàn]

(Mark the boat to find the sword)

有一个楚国人 (the State of Chu)，他坐船 (boat) 要到河的对面去的时候，一不小心 (due to carelessness)，他的剑 (sword) 从他身上掉下去了。

他想把剑捡回来，可是剑已经 (already) 掉进河里去了，怎么办呢? (What should we do?) 那个楚国人，赶快 (hurry) 要他的仆人 (servant) 把他的刀子 (knife) 拿过来，他在船的旁边刻上 (carve) 了一个记号 (mark)。

有人问他：你怎么不下去把剑拿上来呢? 为什么 (why) 在船旁边刻上 (carve) 一个记号 (mark)呢? 那个楚国人指著 (point at) 记号回答 (reply)说：我的剑是从刻这个记号的地方掉下去的，下次我到这儿来的时候，在记号的地方跳下去，就可以把我的剑捞 (scoop up) 上来了。

English translation:

Name: ____________________ Date: ______________

Lesson 21 What Will You Do During the Summer Vacation?

. Listening Exercises

ʟisten and answer in Chinese characters:

ı. ____

ƨ. ____

ȝ. ____

ɬ. ____

I. Character Exercises

ᴀ. For each character, make two phrases, write down the Pinyin, and make a few sentences.

业	毕业 作业	bìyè zuòyè	你今年夏天就要毕业了，对不对？ 我室友常一面做作业一面上网。
班			
打			
假			

B. Write down the radical of each of the following characters and provide the meaning of the radical. List at least five characters that have the same radical:

Example:

Characters	Radical	Meaning of radical	More characters
吗	口	mouth	呢 喝 吃 和 啊
留			
决			
找			
实			
运			

III. Grammar Exercises

Try to state at least six activities by using the following expressions:

(一面……一面…… / 一边……一边……)

我常……

我也喜欢……

Name: ____________________ Date: ______________

V. Comprehensive Exercises

Guided composition: Talk about your plan.

Requirements:

1. *Topic*: Talk about your plans for this summer or for after graduation.
2. Use at least 6 grammar points from the following:

   一面……一面…… / 一边……一边……；了；不……了；就要……了；正在……；然后；以前；以后；得；想；要；会；应该；觉得；把, etc.
3. Write at least 20 sentences.

____

____

____

____

____

____

____

____

Name: ____________________ Date: ______________

Lesson 22 I Have Arrived in Shanghai

. Listening Exercises

A. Listen and mark the correct statements with "✓" and the incorrect ones with "✗":

☐ 1. 我觉得上海的生活很有意思。

☐ 2. 我每天九点起床。

☐ 3. 我的中文老师常常请我去她家玩。

☐ 4. 我常常帮助我的朋友们学中文。

☐ 5. 我们每天要去参观上海的一些地方。

☐ 6. 我的朋友们喜欢每个星期三唱歌。

☐ 7. 上海有很多小吃 [xiǎochī] (snacks)。

☐ 8. 下个星期我们要去美国实习了。

☐ 9. 公司的老板是美国人。

☐ 10. 我们都一定努力工作，多学习。

I. Character Exercises

A. Find five words from the lesson for each of the following categories and write them in characters:

1. People or things

2. Action

3. Time words

4. Descriptive expressions

B. Find one word from each category of Exercise A, then put the words together to make a sentence. If necessary, you may use the word more than once.

1. ______________________________

2. ______________________________

3. ______________________________

4. ______________________________

5. ______________________________

III. Grammar Exercises

A. Find an appropriate measure word from the right column for the phrases in the left column and insert:

一 _____ 报纸	一下儿
两 _____ 运动衫	盘
三 _____ 电脑公司	本
四 _____ 城市	只
五 _____ 课	一点儿
六 _____ 炒面	件
七 _____ 客人	双
八 _____ 汉语书	家
九 _____ 小狗	门
十 _____ 筷子	一会儿
写 _______ 汉字	张
看 _______ 电视	位
我来介绍 _______	个

Note: 一会儿 [yíhuèr]: a short while

Name: ________________ Date: ____________

B. Choose an appropriate conjunction from the following list for each sentence below:

和	还是	因为	可是	不过
虽然	或者	但是	所以	然后

1. 程程到上海已经一个星期了，他还没有给他女朋友打电话。

   ____

2. 他的公司的老板很不错，他很喜欢在这儿工作。

   ____

3. 今年暑假你想去北京的暑期班学习吗？你要去上海的公司实习吗？

   ____

4. 大明最喜欢喝绿茶可乐。

   ____

5. 方文春假想先坐火车再开车去洛杉矶看他的爷爷奶奶。

   ____

6. 我的车是手排挡的，你会开，没问题。

   ____

C. Tell your friend what you like about your university, using 比如 for details, talking about:

1. Your classes.

   ____

2. Your fellow students.

   ____

3. The restaurants near the university.

   ____

IV. Comprehensive Exercises

Guided composition:

You are now studying Chinese in a summer program in Shanghai/Beijing. You are staying at the dorm for foreign students. You have a room of your own. This is the third day after your arrival there. You are writing an email to your parents about your life and studies there. Because this is the first time you are abroad, your parents are very concerned about you. Therefore, you need to provide as many details as possible.

爸爸、妈妈：

我到北京/上海已经三天了。我在这儿都很好，我住在 ……

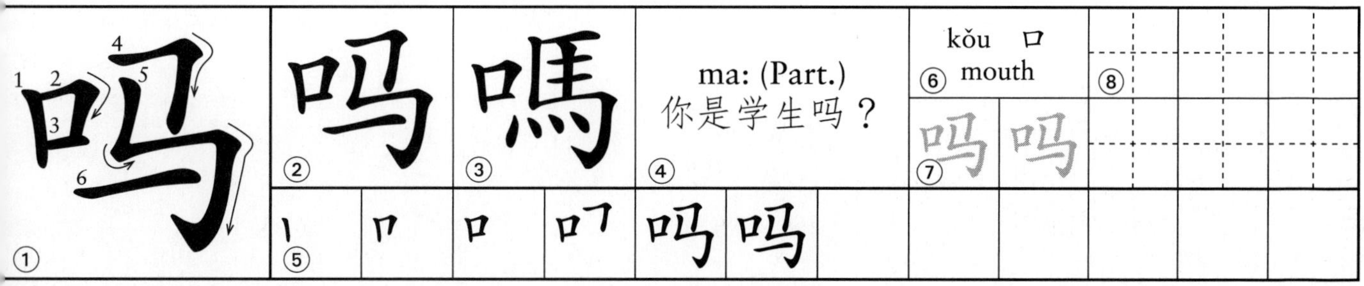

Guide for Students

1) Character with its stroke order indicated by numbers

2) Simplified form of the character

3) Traditional form of the character

4) Pinyin pronunciation, grammatical usage, and example sentence or phrase

5) Stroke order illustrated by writing the character progressively

6) Radical of the character with its Pinyin pronunciation and meaning

7) Ghosted images for students to trace over

8) Dotted graph lines to aid students' practice

Name: ____________________ Date: ______________

Lesson 11 Do You Want Black Tea or Green Tea?

Character	Simplified	Traditional	Meaning	Radical
红	红	紅	hóng: red 红茶	mì 糸 (纟) silk
茶	茶	茶	chá: tea 喝茶	cǎo 艸 (艹) grass
还	还	還	hái: (还是: or) 还是	chuò 辵 (辶) motion
绿	绿	綠	lǜ: green 绿茶	mì 糸 (纟) silk
服	服	服	fú: serve 服务员	ròu 肉 (月) meat

Character	Simplified	Traditional	Meaning	Radical
务	务	務	wù: be engaged in 服务员	lì 力 strength
员	员	員	yuán: person 服务员	kǒu 口 mouth
坐	坐	坐	zuò: sit 请坐	tǔ 土 earth
先	先	先	xiān: (先生: sir, Mr.) 先生	ér 儿 walking man
喝	喝	喝	hē: drink 喝茶	kǒu 口 mouth
杯	杯	杯	bēi: cup 一杯红茶	mù 木 wood

Stroke order:

务: ノ ク 夂 务 务

员: 丶 冖 口 口 吕 员 员

坐: ノ 人 人丿 从 丛 坐 坐

先: ノ 𠂉 牛 生 生 先

喝: 口 口 口 口 口 口 喝 喝 喝 喝

杯: 木 杯

Practice: 务 务 · 员 员 · 坐 坐 · 先 先 · 喝 喝 · 杯 杯

Name: ____________________ Date: ______________

冰	冰	冰	bīng: ice 冰红茶	bīng 冫 ice	丶 冫 … 冰
乐	乐	樂	lè: happy (可乐: Coke) 可乐	piě 丿 left slanted stroke	… 乐
瓶	瓶	瓶	píng: bottle 一瓶	wǎ 瓦 tile	丶 丷 … 并 … 瓶
啤	啤	啤	pí: (啤酒: beer) 啤酒	kǒu 口 mouth	口 … 啤
酒	酒	酒	jiǔ: liquor, wine, alcoholic drink 啤酒	shuǐ 水 (氵) water	氵 … 洒 酒
面	面	麵	miàn: noodle 炒面	yī 一 one	一 … 而 … 面

Character	Simplified	Traditional	Pronunciation and meaning	Radical
饺	饺	餃	jiǎo: dumpling 饺子	shí 食 (饣) food
盘	盘	盤	pán: plate, dish 一盘	mǐn 皿 vessel
炒	炒	炒	chǎo: fry 炒饭	huǒ 火 (灬) fire
十	十	十	shí: ten 十个饺子	shí 十 ten
碗	碗	碗	wǎn: bowl 一碗饭	shí 石 stone
汤	汤	湯	tāng: soup 一碗汤	shuǐ 水 (氵) water

Name: ____________________ Date: ______________

双	双	雙	shuāng: (M.W.) 一双筷子	yòu 又 right hand	
	𠃌	又	双	双	

筷	筷	筷	kuài: chopsticks 筷子	zhú 竹 (⺮) bamboo	
	⺮	竹	筷	筷	筷

Name: ____________________ Date: ______________

Lesson 12 May I Borrow Your Car?

Character	Model	Model	Meaning	Radical	Tracing
借	借	借	jiè: borrow 借车	rén 人(亻) person	借 借
Stroke order:	亻	亻一	亻十	亻廿	亻卄一 借
明	明	明	míng: bright; tomorrow 明天	rì 日 sun	明 明
Stroke order:	日	明			
用	用	用	yòng: use 用车	yòng 用 use	用 用
Stroke order:	丿	冂	月	月	用
得	得	得	děi: have to 我得去接人。	chì 彳 step	得 得
Stroke order:	彳	彳日	彳旦	彳旦一	得 得
场	场	場	chǎng: site, spot (机场: airport) 机场	tǔ 土 earth	场 场
Stroke order:	一	十	土	圴	场 场

Character	Forms	Meaning	Radical
接	接 接	jiē: receive 接人	shǒu 手 (扌) hand
妹	妹 妹	mèi: younger sister 妹妹	nǚ 女 female
飞	飞 飛	fēi: fly 飞机	yǐ 乙 second
玩	玩 玩	wán: play 去玩儿	yù 玉 (王) jade
到	到 到	dào: arrive, reach 到我这儿来	dāo 刀 (刂) knife
排	排 排	pái: (排挡: transmission) 手排挡	shǒu 手 (扌) hand

Name: ____________________ Date: ______________

Character	Traditional	Meaning	Radical
挡	擋	dǎng: gear (排挡: transmission) 手排挡	shǒu 手 (扌) hand
开	開	kāi: drive; open 开车	yī 一 one
应	應	yīng: should 应该	yǎn 广 shelter
该	該	gāi: should 应该	yán 言 (讠) word
题	題	tí: problem; topic 问题	yè 頁 (页) head
白	白	bái: white 白色	bái 白 white

Character	Simplified	Traditional	Meaning / Example	Radical
色	色	色	sè: color 白色	dāo 刀 (刂) knife
停	停	停	tíng: stop; park 停车场	rén 人 (亻) person
习	习	習	xí: practice 练习	bīng 冫 ice
练	练	練	liàn: practice; train 练习	mì 糸 (纟) silk
能	能	能	néng: can; may; be able to 能进步	ròu 肉 (月) meat
进	进	進	jìn: move forward; enter 进步	chuò 辵 (辶) motion

Stroke order: 进: 一 二 井 进

Name: ____________________ Date: ______________

步 (stroke order numbered 1–7)	步	步	bù: step, pace 进步	zhǐ 止 stop

Stroke sequence: 丨 ⺊ 𠃊 止 步 步 步

Name: ____________ Date: ____________

Lesson 13 I Want to Buy a Shirt

Character	Simplified	Traditional	Meaning	Radical
买	买	買	mǎi: buy 买一件衬衫	yǐ 乙 second
衬	衬	襯	chèn: (衬衫: shirt) 衬衫	yī 衣 (衤) clothing
衫	衫	衫	shān: (衬衫: shirt) 衬衫	yī 衣 (衤) clothing
店	店	店	diàn: shop 店员	yǎn 广 shelter
条	条	條	tiáo: (M.W.) 这条裙子	mù 木 wood

裙	裙	裙	qún: skirt 裙子	yī 衣 (衤) clothing

衤 衤㇇ 衤⺕ 衤彐 衤尹 裙

或	或	或	huò: or 或者	gē 戈 spear

一 ㄧ口 ㄧ口一 或 或 或

者	者	者	zhě: (或者: or) 或者	lǎo 耂 old

一 十 土 耂 者

裤	裤	褲	kù: pants 裤子	yī 衣 (衤) clothing

丶 ㇇ 衤 衤 衤 衤丶 衤亠 衤广 衤广 衤庐 衤库 裤

黄	黄	黃	huáng: yellow 黄色	bā 八 eight

一 十 廿 龷 龷 芇 芇 黄 黄 黄 黄

错	错	錯	cuò: wrong: (不错: not bad) 不错	jīn 金 (钅) metal

丿 𠂉 𠂉 𠂉 钅 钅一 针 钳 钳 错 错 错

Name: ________________ Date: ____________

比	比	比	bǐ: compare 比较	bǐ 比 compare
	一	上	比	比

较	较	較	jiào: compare 比较	chē 車 (车) vehicle
	一	车	车	较

穿	穿	穿	chuān: wear 穿裙子	xué 穴 cave
	宀	穴	穿	穿

黑	黑	黑	hēi: black 黑色	hēi 黑 black
	丨	冂	里	黑

试	试	試	shì: try 试试	yán 言 (讠) word
	丶	讠	试	试

帮	帮	幫	bāng: help 帮我看看	jīn 巾 napkin
	一	二	三	帮

Character	Simplified	Traditional	Meaning	Radical
让	让	讓	ràng: let 让我看看。	yán 言 (讠) word
钱	钱	錢	qián: money 多少钱？	jīn 金 (钅) metal
块	块	塊	kuài: (money) yuan; piece 十五块钱	tǔ 土 earth
张	张	張	zhāng: (M.W.) 一张票	gōng 弓 bow
影	影	影	yǐng: movie, picture 电影	shān 彡 fur
票	票	票	piào: ticket 电影票	shì 示 (礻) reveal

Name: ____________ Date: ____________

Lesson 14 I Am 20 This Year

岁	岁	歲	suì: year (of age) 二十岁	xī 夕 night
	丨 山 山 屮 岁 岁			岁 岁

空	空	空	kòng: free time 你有没有空？	xué 穴 cave
	宀 宂 穴 空			空 空

星	星	星	xīng: star (星期: week) 星期一	rì 日 sun
	日 星			星 星

过	过	過	guò: spend 过生日	chuò 辵(辶) motion
	一 寸 寸 寸 讨 过			过 过

为	为	為	wèi: for 为我	diǎn 丶 dot
	丶 ソ 为 为			为 为

舞	舞	舞	wǔ: dance (舞会: dancing party) 舞会	piě 丿 left slanted stroke
Stroke order:	𠂉	𠂉	無	舞

Stroke order: 𠂉 ⺈ 㒳 無 無 舞 舞 舞 舞 舞

参	参	参	cān: join (参加: attend) 参加	sī 厶 private

Stroke order: 𠃋 厶 厽 叁 参 参 参 参

加	加	加	jiā: add (参加: attend) 参加	lì 力 strength

Stroke order: 乛 力 加 加 加

定	定	定	dìng: surely 一定	mián 宀 roof

Stroke order: 宀 宀 宁 宁 定 定

蛋	蛋	蛋	dàn: egg 蛋糕	chóng 虫 insect

Stroke order: 乛 丆 下 疋 疋 疋 蛋 蛋 蛋 蛋 蛋

糕	糕	糕	gāo: cake 蛋糕	mǐ 米 rice

Stroke order: 丶 丷 丷 半 米 米 米 糕 糕 糕 糕 糕

Name: ____________________ Date: ______________

送	送	送	sòng: give as a present 送你一个蛋糕	chuò 辵(辶) motion 送 送										
	丶	丷	䒑	兰	关	关	关	送						

棒	棒	棒	bàng: good, excellent 太棒了！	mù 木 wood 棒 棒							
	木	朩	朩	朩	栱	栱	棒	棒	棒		

客	客	客	kè: guest, visitor (客气: polite; modest) 不客气！	mián 宀 roof 客 客							
	宀	宂	宊	安	客						

气	气	氣	qì: air (客气: polite; modest) 不客气！	qì 气 air 气 气							
	丿	𠂉	气	气							

Name: ____________________ Date: ______________

Lesson 15 The Library Is in Front of the Dorm

前	前	前	qián: front 前边	dāo 刀 (刂) knife 前 前		
	丶	丷	䒑	䒑月	前	前

边	边	邊	biān: (前边: front) 前边	chuò 辵 (辶) motion 边 边		
	㇇	力	丶力	辶力	边	

迎	迎	迎	yíng: greet 欢迎	chuò 辵 (辶) motion 迎 迎		
	㇒	𠂆	卬	卬	迎	

观	观	觀	guān: observe, look at 参观	jiàn 見 (见) see 观 观		
	㇇	又	又丨	又冂	观	观

里	里	裡	lǐ: inside 里边	lǐ 里 inside 里 里			
	丨	冂	日	日	旦	甲	里

Character	Traditional	Meaning	Word	Radical
厨	廚	chú: kitchen	厨房	hàn 厂 shelter
公	公	gōng: public	公用	bā 八 eight
旁	旁	páng: side	旁边	fāng 方 square
走	走	zǒu: walk	走路	zǒu 走 walk
厅	廳	tīng: hall	客厅	hàn 厂 shelter
面	面	miàn: opposite	对面	yī 一 one

Name: ____________________ Date: ______________

Character	Simplified / Traditional	Meaning	Radical
餐	餐 餐	cān: meal, food 餐厅	shí 食 (饣) food
洗	洗 洗	xǐ: wash 洗澡间	shuǐ 水 (氵) water
澡	澡 澡	zǎo: bath 洗澡	shuǐ 水 (氵) water
卧	卧 臥	wò: lie 卧室	chén 臣 official
桌	桌 桌	zhuō: desk, table 桌子	mù 木 wood
园	园 園	yuán: a piece of land 公园	wéi 口 enclosure

真	真	真	zhēn: really, truly 真不错	shí 十 ten
一 十	真			

Name: ____________________ Date: ______________

Lesson 16 She Plays Basketball Very Well

Character			Meaning	Radical
篮	篮	籃	lán: basket 篮球	zhú 竹 (⺮) bamboo
俩	俩	倆	liǎ: two 你们俩	rén 人 (亻) person
教	教	教	jiào/jiāo: teach 教练/教得很好	pū 攴 (攵) literacy
游	游	游	yóu: swim 游泳游得很快	shuǐ 水 (氵) water
泳	泳	泳	yǒug: swim 游泳	shuǐ 水 (氵) water

Character	Forms	Meaning	Radical
非	非 非	fēi: wrong: not (非常: extraordinary, unusual) 非常	gǔn 丨 down stroke
快	快 快	kuài: fast 很快	xīn 心 (忄) heart
体	体 體	tǐ: body 体育	rén 人 (亻) person
育	育 育	yù: educate 体育	ròu 肉 (月) meat
池	池 池	chí: pool 游泳池	shuǐ 水 (氵) water
健	健 健	jiàn: strengthen; healthy 健身房	rén 人 (亻) person

Name: ____________________ Date: ______________

Character	Simplified	Traditional	Meaning	Word	Radical
身	身	身	shēn: body	健身房	shēn 身 body
锻	锻	鍛	duàn: forge	锻炼	jīn 金 (钅) metal
炼	炼	煉	liàn: refine	锻炼	huǒ 火 (灬) fire
现	现	現	xiàn: now	现在	yù 玉 (王) jade
昨	昨	昨	zuó: yesterday	昨天	rì 日 sun
赛	赛	賽	sài: game, match	球赛	bèi 貝 (贝) shell

业	业	業	yè: course of study (作业: homework) 作业	yè 业 board
	丨 丨丨 丨丨丶 丨丨丶丿 业			

包	包	包	bāo: wrap 包饺子	bāo 勹 wrap
	丿 勹 勺 匀 包			

慢	慢	慢	màn: slow 很慢	xīn 心 (忄) heart
	忄 忄曰 㥄 慢 慢			

Name: ____________________ Date: ______________

Lesson 17 Spring Is Coming Soon

Character	Meaning	Radical
春	chūn: spring 春天	rì 日 sun
久	jiǔ: long 好久不见	piě 丿 left slanted stroke
放	fàng: put, release, let go 放假	pū 攴(攵) literacy
假	jià: vacation, holiday 春假	rén 人(亻) person
夏	xià: summer 夏天	zhǐ 夂 from the end

Character	Pinyin / Meaning	Example	Radical
秋	qiū: fall, autumn	秋天	hé 禾 grain
冬	dōng: winter	冬天	bīng 冫 ice
其	qí: that, such (其中: among which; whom)	其中	qí 其 he
最	zuì: most	最喜欢	yuē 曰 say
暖	nuǎn: warm	暖和	rì 日 sun
短	duǎn: short	很短	shǐ 矢 arrow

Name: ____________________ Date: ______________

Character	Traditional	Pronunciation and meaning	Example	Radical
热	熱	rè: hot	非常热	huǒ 火 (灬) fire
华	華	huá: (华氏: Fahrenheit)	华氏	shí 十 ten
氏	氏	shì: (华氏: Fahrenheit)	华氏	piě 丿 left slanted stroke
百	百	bǎi: hundred	华氏一百度	bái 白 white
度	度	dù: degree	华氏一百度	yǎn 广 shelter
极	極	jí: extreme	热极了	mù 木 wood

刮	刮	刮	guā: blow 刮风	dāo 刀 (刂) knife

㇐ 二 千 舌 刮 刮

风	风	風	fēng: wind 刮风	fēng 风 wind

丿 几 风 风

雨	雨	雨	yǔ: rain 下雨	yǔ 雨 rain

一 丅 冂 币 帀 雨 雨 雨

冷	冷	冷	lěng: cold 非常冷	bīng 冫 ice

冫 冫 冫 冷 冷

雪	雪	雪	xuě: snow 下雪	yǔ 雨 rain

一 冖 雨 雨 雨 雨 雨 雪 雪 雪

Name: ____________________ Date: ______________

Lesson 18 We Are Going to Take a Train Trip

火

火	火	火	huǒ: fire (火车: train) 火车	huǒ 火 (灬) fire	火	火

Stroke order: 丶 丷 火 火

旅

旅	旅	旅	lǚ: travel 旅行	fāng 方 square	旅	旅

Stroke order: 方 方 方 方 方 旅

离

离	离	離	lí: leave, part from, away 离学校不远	tóu 亠 cover	离	离

Stroke order: 丶 亠 亠 文 文 这 这 离 离 离

远

远	远	遠	yuǎn: far, distant 不远	chuò 辵 (辶) motion	远	远

Stroke order: 一 二 テ 元 元 沅 远

只

只	只	只	zhǐ: only 只要	kǒu 口 mouth	只	只

Stroke order: 口 只 只

钟 鐘

zhōng: clock
分钟

jīn 金 (钅)
metal

钟 钟

骑 騎

qí: ride
骑自行车

mǎ 馬 (马)
horse

骑 骑

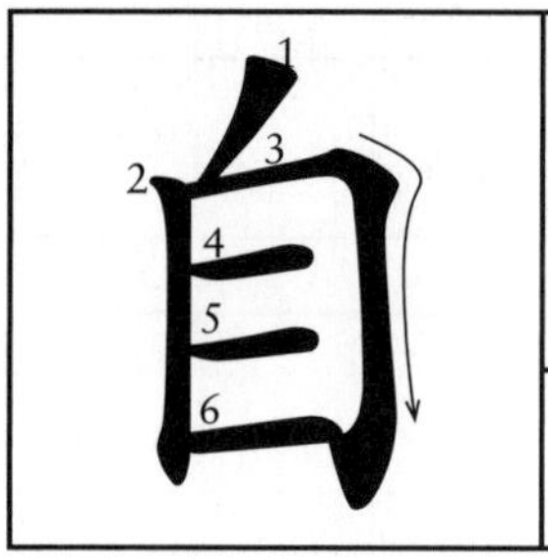

自 自

zì: self
自行车

zì 自
self

自 自

共 共

gòng: common, general
公共汽车

bā 八
eight

共 共

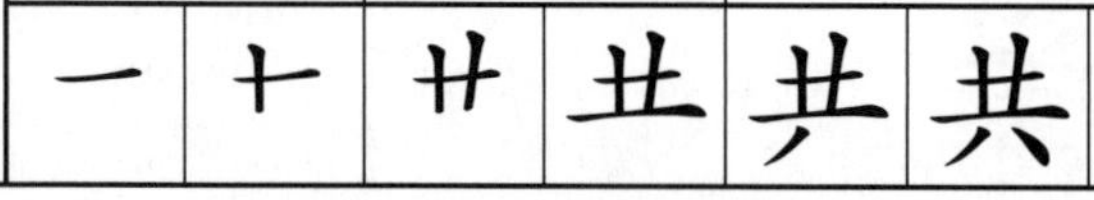

汽 汽

qì: steam, vapor
汽车

shuǐ 水 (氵)
water

汽 汽

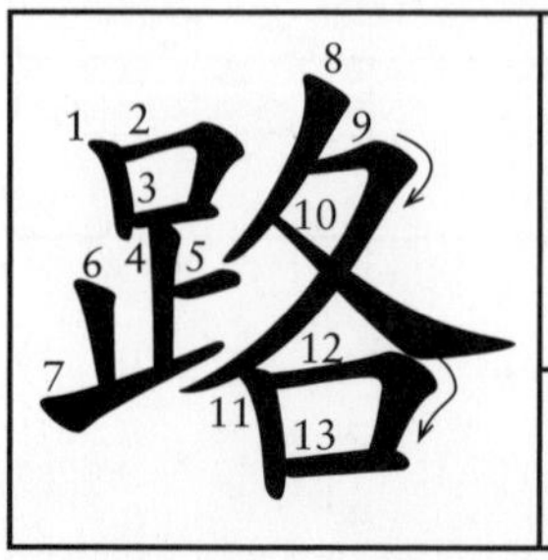

路 路

lù: road
走路

zú 足
foot

路 路

Name: ____________________ Date: ______________

Character	Meaning	Example	Radical
近	jìn: near, close	很近	chuò 辵(辶) motion
西	xī: west	西部	xī 西 perch
部	bù: part	西部	yì 邑(阝) city
景	jǐng: view, scenery	风景	rì 日 sun
船	chuán: boat, ship	坐船	zhōu 舟 boat
南	nán: south	南部	shí 十 ten

听	听	聽	tīng: listen 听说	kǒu 口 mouth 听 听
	丨 ㄇ 口 口′ 叮 吓 听			

海	海	海	hǎi: sea 海边	shuǐ 水(氵) water 海 海
	氵 氵 氵 汇 海 海 海 海			

租	租	租	zū: rent 租车	hé 禾 grain 租 租
	禾 利 和 和 租 租			

Name: ____________________ Date: ______________

Lesson 19 I Caught a Cold

Character			Meaning	Radical
感	感	感	gǎn: feel, sense (感冒: cold; catch a cold) 感冒	xīn 心 (忄) heart
冒	冒	冒	mào: emit, give off (感冒: cold; catch a cold) 感冒	yuē 曰 say
饿	饿	餓	è: hungry 我不饿。	shí 食 (饣) food
像	像	像	xiàng: be like; seem 好像	rén 人 (亻) person
舒	舒	舒	shū: loosen, relax 舒服	rén 人 (亻) person

Character	Simplified	Traditional	Meaning	Radical	Stroke order
头	头	頭	tóu: head 头疼	zhǔ 丶 segmentation symbol	丶 ⺀ ㇀ 头 头
疼	疼	疼	téng: ache; pain 头疼	nè 疒 sick	丶 亠 广 疒 疒 疼
发	发	發	fā: feel; send out 发烧	yòu 又 right hand	𠃋 ⺦ 方 发 发
烧	烧	燒	shāo: fever 发烧	huǒ 火 (灬) fire	丶 丷 火 火 火 炏 炏 烧 烧 烧
咳	咳	咳	ké: cough 咳嗽	kǒu 口 mouth	口 咳
嗽	嗽	嗽	sòu: (咳嗽: cough) 咳嗽	kǒu 口 mouth	口 口 口 口 口 口 口 口 口 嗽

Name: ____________________ Date: ______________

Character			Meaning	Radical
病	病	病	bìng: be taken ill; disease 生病	nè 疒 sick

Stroke order: 疒 疒 疒 疔 病 病

Character			Meaning	Radical
考	考	考	kǎo: give or take an exam, a test or a quiz 考试	lǎo 耂 old

Stroke order: 一 十 土 耂 耂 考

Character			Meaning	Radical
复	复	復	fù: repeat (复习: review) 复习	pū 攴(攵) literacy

Stroke order: 丿 𠂉 𠂉 𠂉 𠂉 𠂉 复 复 复

Character			Meaning	Radical
所	所	所	suǒ: (所以: therefore) 所以	jīn 斤 axe

Stroke order: ㇀ 厂 户 户 户 所 所 所

Character			Meaning	Radical
医	医	醫	yī: doctor; medical science 医生	fāng 匚 square vessel

Stroke order: 一 丆 𠂇 𠂇 𠂇 医 医

Character			Meaning	Radical
药	药	藥	yào: medicine 吃药	cǎo 艸(艹) grass

Stroke order: 一 十 艹 艹 艹 艹 艹 药 药

Character	Simplified	Traditional	Meaning	Radical
休	休	休	xiū: rest 休息	rén 人 (亻) person
息	息	息	xī: rest (休息: xiūxi) 休息	xīn 心 (忄) heart
准	准	準	zhǔn: (准备: prepare; plan) 准备	bīng 冫 ice
备	备	備	bèi: prepare, get ready 准备	zhǐ 夂 from the end
笔	笔	筆	bǐ: notes; record 笔记	zhú 竹 (⺮) bamboo
记	记	記	jì: notes; record 笔记	yán 言 (讠) word

Stroke order:

休: 亻 仁 什 什 休

息: 丿 自 息

准: 丶 冫 丷 汁 汁 汻 汻 准 准 准

备: 丿 ク 夂 冬 各 各 备 备

笔: 丿 𠂉 𥫗 𥫗 𥫗 ⺮ 笋 笔 笔 笔

记: 丶 讠 讠 订 记

Name: ____________________ Date: ______________

Lesson 20 I've Brought Xiao Xie Over . . .

Character	Meaning / Example	Radical	Stroke order
把	bǎ: (Prep.) 我把车开回来了。	shǒu 手 (扌) hand	扌 … 把
带	dài: bring 带来	jīn 巾 napkin	一 … 带
啊	a: (Int.) 是小谢啊！	kǒu 口 mouth	口 … 啊
搬	bān: move 搬出去	shǒu 手 (扌) hand	扌 … 搬
出	chū: out 搬出去	kǎn 凵 hole	… 出

Character	Simplified	Traditional	Meaning	Radical	Stroke order
吸	吸	吸	xī: inhale 吸烟	kǒu 口 mouth	丨 ㄇ 口 口丿 吸 吸
烟	烟	煙	yān: smoke; cigarette 吸烟	huǒ 火 (灬) fire	丶 丷 少 火 火丨 灯 炣 炣 烟 烟
关	关	關	guān: concern 关系	bā 八 eight	丶 丷 丷 兰 关 关
系	系	係	xì: relate to 关系	mì 糸 silk	一 乙 乡 幺 系 系 系
但	但	但	dàn: but 但是	rén 人 (亻) person	亻 伯 但
女	女	女	nǚ: female 女朋友	nǚ 女 female	乛 女 女

Name: ____________________ Date: ______________

必	必	必	bì: must, have to 必须	xīn 心 (忄) heart	必 必

丶 心 心 必 必

须	须	須	xū: must, have to 必须	yè 頁 (页) head	须 须

丿 彡 彡 彡 彡 彡 须 须 须

第	第	第	dì: (prefix for ordinal numbers) 第一天	zhú 竹 (⺮) bamboo	第 第

⺮ 笃 笃 笃 第 第

付	付	付	fù: pay 付房租	rén 人 (亻) person	付 付

亻 仁 付 付

楼	楼	樓	lóu: floor 楼上	mù 木 wood	楼 楼

一 十 才 木 木 木 木 杪 杪 楼 楼

马	马	馬	mǎ: horse (马上: at once) 马上	mǎ 馬 (马) horse	马 马

㇇ 马 马

Name: ____________________ Date: ______________

Lesson 21 What Will You Do During the Summer Vacation?

Character	Forms	Meaning	Example	Radical
暑	暑 暑	shǔ: heat, hot weather	暑假	rì 日 sun
毕	毕 畢	bì: finish, accomplish	毕业	bǐ 比 compare
决	决 決	jué: decide	决定	bīng 冫 ice
申	申 申	shēn: state, express	申请	tián 田 land
研	研 研	yán: study	研究	shí 石 stone

Character	Traditional	Meaning	Radical
究	究	jiū: study carefully; investigate 研究	xué 穴 cave
院	院	yuàn: institute 研究院	fù 阜 (阝) hill
找	找	zhǎo: look for 找工作	shǒu 手 (扌) hand
司	司	sī: department 公司	kǒu 口 mouth
实	實	shí: solid; true (实习: intern) 实习	mián 宀 roof
脑	腦	nǎo: brain 电脑	ròu 肉 (月) moon

Name: ______________ Date: ______________

Character			Meaning	Radical
班	班	班	bān: class 暑期班	yù 玉 (王) jade
意	意	意	yì: meaning 意思	xīn 心 (忄) heart
思	思	思	sī: think, consider (意思: yìsi) 有意思	xīn 心 (忄) heart
愉	愉	愉	yú: happy 愉快	xīn 心 (忄) heart
平	平	平	píng: calm, peaceful 平安	yī 一 one
安	安	安	ān: safe 平安	mián 宀 roof

运 (stroke order 1–7)	运	運	yùn: luck 好运	chuò 辵(辶) motion 运 运
	一 二 云 云 云 运 运			

Name: ____________________ Date: ______________

Lesson 22 I Have Arrived in Shanghai

Character	Simplified	Traditional	Meaning	Radical
因	因	因	yīn: because 因为	wéi 囗 enclosure
已	已	已	yǐ: already (已经: already) 已经	jǐ 己 self
经	经	經	jīng: pass (已经: already) 已经	mì 糸 (纟) silk
丽	丽	麗	lì: beautiful 美丽	yī 一 one
城	城	城	chéng: city 城市	tǔ 土 earth

Character	Forms	Meaning	Radical	Stroke order
市	市 市	shì: city 城市	jīn 巾 napkin	丶 亠 亠 冂 市
处	处 處	chù: place 到处	zhǐ 夂 from the end	丿 ク 夂 夂 处
新	新 新	xīn: new 新的大楼	jīn 斤 ax	丶 亠 亠 亠 立 立 辛 辛 亲 新 新 新
些	些 些	xiē: some 一些	bǐ 匕 dagger	丨 卜 止 止 止 此 此 些
方	方 方	fāng: direction; side 地方	fāng 方 place	丶 亠 亠 方
动	动 動	dòng: move 活动	lì 力 strength	一 二 亍 云 动 动

Name: ________________ Date: ____________

如	如	如	rú: be like; as if 比如	nǚ 女 female
				如 如

Stroke order: 女 如

京	京	京	jīng: Beijing; the capital of a country 京剧	tóu 亠 cover
				京 京

Stroke order: 丶 亠 亠口 亠口亅 亠口亅丿 京

剧	剧	劇	jù: opera, play, drama 京剧	dāo 刀 (刂) knife
				剧 剧

Stroke order: 丿 厂 尸 尸 屏 屏 居 居 居 剧

东	东	東	dōng: east (东西: thing) 东西	yī 一 one
				东 东

Stroke order: 一 七 车 东 东

笼	笼	籠	lóng: cage; steamer 小笼包	zhú 竹 (⺮) bamboo
				笼 笼

Stroke order: 丿 𠂉 𠂉 𠂉丿 𠂉𠂉 ⺮ ⺮ 笋 笼 笼 笼

尝	尝	嚐	cháng: taste 尝尝	xiǎo 小 little
				尝 尝

Stroke order: 丨 丨丶 ⺌ ⺌ 𫩠 𫩠 尝 尝 尝

Character	Simplified	Traditional	Meaning	Radical
始	始	始	shǐ: beginning 开始	nǚ 女 female
高	高	高	gāo: high 高兴	tóu 亠 cover
兴	兴	興	xìng: pleasure 高兴	bā 八 eight
收	收	收	shōu: receive 收到	pū 攴(攵) literacy
心	心	心	xīn: heart 开心	xīn 心(忄) heart
板	板	闆	bǎn: board, plate (老板: boss) 老板	mù 木 wood

Stroke order:

- 始: 女 女厶 女厶 始
- 高: 丶 亠 亠口 亠口丨 高 高
- 兴: 丶 丷 ⺍ 䒑 兴 兴
- 收: 丩 丩 收 收 收 收
- 心: 丶 心 心 心
- 板: 一 十 才 木 木ノ 杤 枋 板

Name: ____________ Date: ____________

保	保	保	bǎo: protect; maintain 保重	rén 人 (亻) person	
	亻 亻 伻 伻 保 保 保			保 保	

重	重	重	zhòng: heavy 保重	lǐ 里 hamlet	
	一 二 千 千 斤 肓 肓 重 重			重 重	

写字簿生词索引 CHARACTER BOOK INDEX (BY NUMBER OF STROKES)

Each entry lists simplified character, traditional character, Pinyin, English meaning, and lesson number.

1

2

3

4

9

13

14

15

16

写字簿生词索引 CHARACTER BOOK INDEX (BY LESSON NUMBER)

Each entry lists simplified character, traditional character, Pinyin, and English meaning.

Lesson 1

你		nǐ	you
好		hǎo	good
是		shì	is, are
学	學	xué	study
生		shēng	student
吗	嗎	ma	Part.
我		wǒ	I, me
呢		ne	Part.
也		yě	also, too
他		tā	he, him
不		bù	not
老		lǎo	old
师	師	shī	teacher

Lesson 2

您		nín	(polite) you
贵	貴	guì	noble, honored
姓		xìng	family name
请	請	qǐng	please
问	問	wèn	ask
的		de	Part.
英		yīng	英文: English
文		wén	language, writing
名		míng	name
字		zì	character, word
中		zhōng	middle
叫		jiào	call
什		shén	什么: what
么	麼	me	什么: what
她		tā	she, her
谁	誰	shéi	who, whom
同		tóng	same, similar

Lesson 3

哪		nǎ	which
国	國	guó	country
人		rén	person
很		hěn	very
对	對	duì	correct
了		le	Part.
法		fǎ	法国: France
美		měi	beautiful
说	說	shuō	speak
会	會	huì	be able to
一		yī	one
点	點	diǎn	dot
儿	兒	ér	(retroflex ending)
和		hé	and

Lesson 4

那		nà	that
书	書	shū	book
这	這	zhè	this
本		běn	M.W.
工		gōng	work
程		chéng	工程: engineering
难	難	nán	difficult
太		tài	too
可		kě	but
功		gōng	功课: homework
课	課	kè	class
多		duō	many, much
们	們	men	(suffix)
少		shǎo	few, little

Lesson 5

朋		péng	friend
友		yǒu	friend
来	來	lái	come
介		jiè	介绍: introduce
绍	紹	shào	介绍: introduce
下		xià	down; get off
室		shì	room
有		yǒu	have
几	幾	jǐ	how many
两	兩	liǎng	two
个	個	gè	M.W.
都		dōu	all; both
常		cháng	often
跟		gēn	with

Lesson 6

家		jiā	home
大		dà	big
从	從	cóng	from
在		zài	at, in
四		sì	four
爸		bà	dad
妈	媽	mā	mom
姐		jiě	older sister
作		zuò	工作: work
男		nán	male
没	沒	méi	don't have
辆	輛	liàng	M.W. for vehicles
车	車	chē	car
只	隻	zhī	M.W.
狗		gǒu	dog
爱	愛	ài	love

Lesson 7

住		zhù	live
宿		sù	stay overnight
舍		shè	house
号	號	hào	number
房		fáng	house
间	間	jiān	room
电	電	diàn	electricity
话	話	huà	word
小		xiǎo	small
码	碼	mǎ	number
二		èr	two
三		sān	three
五		wǔ	five
六		liù	six
七		qī	seven
八		bā	eight
九		jiǔ	nine
手		shǒu	hand
机	機	jī	machine
校		xiào	school
外		wài	outside

Lesson 8

认	認	rèn	know, recognize
识	識	shí	know, recognize
去		qù	go
上		shàng	get on, attend
以		yǐ	以后: after, later
后	後	hòu	behind
事		shì	matter, thing
想		xiǎng	want, think
回		huí	return
起		qǐ	一起: together
吃		chī	eat
饭	飯	fàn	rice, meal
菜		cài	dish
今		jīn	today
天		tiān	day
次		cì	order, sequence
怎		zěn	how
样	樣	yàng	appearance
行		xíng	okay
再		zài	again
见	見	jiàn	see

Lesson 9

打		dǎ	hit, play, make
喂		wèi/wéi	hello, hey
等		děng	wait

知		zhī	know
道		dào	road, walk
谢	謝	xiè	thanks
吧		ba	Part.
忙		máng	busy
正		zhèng	in process of
看		kàn	see, watch
视	視	shì	look
做		zuò	do
网	網	wǎng	net
就		jiù	Adv.
位		wèi	M.W.
留		liú	leave, remain
言		yán	speech, words
时	時	shí	time
候		hòu	time
晚		wǎn	night, late
要		yào	want
给	給	gěi	give; for, to

Lesson 10

活		huó	live
期		qī	a period of time
门	門	mén	M.W.
每		mei	every, each
床		chuáng	bed
睡		shuì	sleep
觉	覺	jiào	sleep
半		bàn	half
才		cái	Adv.
刻		kè	a quarter
分		fēn	minute
然		rán	然后: then
图	圖	tú	picture
馆	館	guǎn	house, hall
午		wǔ	noon
喜		xǐ	happy; like
欢	歡	huān	joyfully
球		qiú	ball
写	寫	xiě	write
信		xìn	letter
子		zǐ	(suffix)
邮	郵	yóu	mail
件		jiàn	letter
地		dì	land
址		zhǐ	location
祝		zhù	wish
年		nián	year
月		yuè	month
日		rì	day

Lesson 11

红	紅	hóng	red
茶		chá	tea
还	還	hái	还是: or
绿	綠	lǜ	green
服		fú	serve
务	務	wù	be engaged in
员	員	yuán	person
坐		zuò	sit
先		xiān	先生: sir, Mr.
喝		hē	drink
杯		bēi	cup
冰		bīng	ice
乐	樂	lè	happy
瓶		píng	bottle
啤		pí	beer
酒		jiǔ	liquor
面	麵	miàn	noodle
饺	餃	jiǎo	dumpling
盘	盤	pán	plate
炒		chǎo	fry
十		shí	ten
碗		wǎn	bowl
汤	湯	tāng	soup
双	雙	shuāng	pair
筷		kuài	chopsticks

Lesson 12

借		jiè	borrow
明		míng	tomorrow
用		yòng	use
得		děi	have to
场	場	chǎng	site
接		jiē	receive

妹		mèi	younger sister
飞	飛	fēi	fly
玩		wán	play
到		dào	arrive
排		pái	line
挡	擋	dǎng	gear
开	開	kāi	drive
应	應	yīng	should
该	該	gāi	should
题	題	tí	problem, topic
白		bái	white
色		sè	color
停		tíng	stop, park
习	習	xí	practice
练	練	liàn	practice
能		néng	can, may
进	進	jìn	move forward
步		bù	step

Lesson 13

买	買	mǎi	buy
衬	襯	chèn	衬衫: shirt
衫		shān	shirt, clothes
店		diàn	shop
条	條	tiáo	M.W.
裙		qún	skirt
或		huò	or
者		zhě	或者: or
裤	褲	kù	pants
黄	黃	huáng	yellow
错	錯	cuò	wrong
比		bǐ	compare
较	較	jiào	compare
穿		chuān	wear
黑		hēi	black
试	試	shì	try
帮	幫	bāng	help
让	讓	ràng	let
钱	錢	qián	money
块	塊	kuài	dollar
张	張	zhāng	M.W.
影		yǐng	shadow, movie
票		piào	ticket

Lesson 14

岁	歲	suì	year (of age)
空		kòng	free time
星		xīng	star
过	過	guò	spend
为	為	wèi	for
舞		wǔ	dance
参	參	cān	join
加		jiā	add
定		dìng	surely
蛋		dàn	egg
糕		gāo	cake
送		sòng	give as a present
棒		bàng	good, excellent
客		kè	guest
气	氣	qì	air

Lesson 15

前		qián	front
边	邊	biān	side
迎		yíng	greet
观	觀	guān	observe
里	裡	lǐ	inside
厨	廚	chú	kitchen
公		gōng	public
旁		páng	side
走		zǒu	walk
厅	廳	tīng	hall
面		miàn	surface
餐		cān	meal, food
洗		xǐ	wash
澡		zǎo	bath
卧	臥	wò	lie
桌		zhuō	table
园	園	yuán	a piece of land
真		zhēn	really

Lesson 16

篮	籃	lán	basket
俩	倆	liǎ	two
教		jiào/jiāo	teach

游		yóu	swim
泳		yǒng	swim
非		fēi	wrong, not
快		kuài	fast
体	體	tǐ	body
育		yù	educate
池		chí	pool
健		jiàn	healthy
身		shēn	body
锻	鍛	duàn	forge
炼	煉	liàn	refine
现	現	xiàn	now
昨		zuó	yesterday
赛	賽	sài	game, match
业	業	yè	course of study
包		bāo	wrap
慢		màn	slow

Lesson 17

春		chūn	spring
久		jiǔ	long
放		fàng	put, release
假		jià	vacation
夏		xià	summer
秋		qiū	fall, autumn
冬		dōng	winter
其		qí	that, such
最		zuì	most
暖		nuǎn	warm
短		duǎn	short
热	熱	rè	hot
华	華	huá	华氏: Fahrenheit
氏		shì	华氏: Fahrenheit
百		bǎi	hundred
度		dù	degree
极	極	jí	extreme
刮		guā	blow
风	風	fēng	wind
雨		yǔ	rain
冷		lěng	cold
雪		xuě	snow

Lesson 18

火		huǒ	fire
旅		lǚ	travel
离	離	lí	leave, part from
远	遠	yuǎn	far
只		zhǐ	only
钟	鐘	zhōng	clock
骑	騎	qí	ride
自		zì	self
共		gòng	common
汽		qì	steam
路		lù	road
近		jìn	close
西		xī	west
部		bù	part
景		jǐng	view, scenery
船		chuán	boat, ship
南		nán	south
听	聽	tīng	listen
海		hǎi	sea
租		zū	rent

Lesson 19

感		gǎn	feel, sense
冒		mào	emit, give off
饿	餓	è	hungry
像		xiàng	be like; seem
舒		shū	loosen, relax
头	頭	tóu	head
疼		téng	ache, pain
发	發	fā	feel, send out
烧	燒	shāo	fever
咳		ké	cough
嗽		sòu	cough
病		bìng	sick
考		kǎo	give or take a test
复	復	fù	repeat
所		suǒ	所以: therefore
医	醫	yī	medical science
药	藥	yào	medicine
休		xiū	休息: rest

息		xī	rest
准	準	zhǔn	prepare
备	備	bèi	prepare
笔	筆	bǐ	pen
记	記	jì	notes

Lesson 20

把		bǎ	Prep.
带	帶	dài	bring
啊		a	Int.
搬		bān	move
出		chū	out
吸		xī	inhale
烟	煙	yān	smoke
关	關	guān	concern
系	係	xì	relate to
但		dàn	but
女		nǚ	female
必		bì	must
须	須	xū	must
第		dì	(prefix)
付		fù	pay
楼	樓	lóu	floor
马	馬	mǎ	horse

Lesson 21

暑		shǔ	heat, hot
毕	畢	bì	finish
决	決	jué	decide
申		shēn	express
研		yán	study
究		jiū	study
院		yuàn	institute
找		zhǎo	look for
司		sī	department
实	實	shí	solid
脑	腦	nǎo	brain
班		bān	class
意		yì	meaning
思		sī	think
愉		yú	happy
平		píng	calm, peaceful
安		ān	safe
运	運	yùn	luck

Lesson 22

因		yīn	because
已		yǐ	already
经	經	jīng	pass
丽	麗	lì	beautiful
城		chéng	city
市		shì	city
处	處	chù	place
新		xīn	new
些		xiē	some
方		fāng	side, direction
动	動	dòng	move
如		rú	be like
京		jīng	capital
剧	劇	jù	opera, drama
东	東	dōng	east
笼	籠	lóng	cage, steamer
尝	嚐	cháng	taste
始		shǐ	beginning
高		gāo	high
兴	興	xìng	pleasure
收		shōu	receive
心		xīn	heart
板	闆	bǎn	老板: boss
保		bǎo	protect, maintain
重		zhòng	heavy

写字簿生词索引 CHARACTER BOOK INDEX (ALPHABETICAL BY PINYIN)

Each entry lists simplified character, traditional character, Pinyin, English meaning, and lesson number.

L

M

Y

Z

Name: ____________________ Date: ______________

Name: ____________________ Date: ______________

Name: ____________________ Date: ______________

Name: ____________________ Date: ______________

Name: ____________________ Date: ______________

Name: ____________________ Date: ______________

Name: ____________________ Date: ______________

Name: ____________________ Date: ______________

Name: ____________________ Date: ______________

Name: ____________________ Date: ______________

Name: ____________________ Date: ______________

Name: ____________________ Date: ______________

Name: ____________________ Date: ______________

Name: ____________________ Date: ______________

Name: ____________________ Date: ______________